Miss Phillips, You Were Wrong

A Formula To Handle Rejection

Peter J Daniels

Miss Phillips, You Were Wrong
Copyright © 1989 by Peter J. Daniels
National Library of Australia card number
and ISBN 0 949330 26 4

The author would like to thank Geoff Strelan for his valued
assistance in the writing of this book.

Cover photos by Greg Steer.

Printed and bound in Australia
by Gillingham Printers of Adelaide, South Australia.

Published by **The House of Tabor**
  Lynton Avenue,
  South Plympton, South Australia 5043.

in co-operation with
World Centre for Entrepreneurial Studies
38–40 Carrington Street, Adelaide, South Australia, Australia, 5000
Telephone: 61-8-231 0111
Facsimile: 61-8-211 8423

This book is dedicated to
Dr Norman Vincent Peale, who
blazed the trail for us all, by
proving the sceptics wrong.

Contents

Preface

I was about seven years of age when I arrived at the new school and everything seemed strange and scary. My mother had really been responsible for our shift from the west end of Adelaide to the north Adelaide area. She felt it was a better district and therefore a move that could only have a positive effect.

World War II had just started and the army of Adolf Hitler, the Chancellor of Germany, had marched on Poland. The great Depression was coming to an end; my father had finally obtained permanent work as a factory hand at General Motors Holden and the future must have looked a little better.

I had come out of hospital about a year earlier. I had spent a very long time fighting for my life against the dreaded disease of that time — diphtheria. I was still suffering from the effects of being ill for so long and the debilitating disease had left me skinny, weak and delicate. It seemed I had constant headaches and was susceptible to any malady that came along.

The nights were the worst because of the

reoccurring nightmares which were to haunt me for the rest of my life. I would be lying helplessly in bed and people dressed in white would put needles into me. I felt that I was in a furnace and then everything would go quiet and peaceful until the burning and the pain came again. My mother told me that one particular night I was not expected to pull through.

My introduction to the new school came by meeting the head mistress, Miss Thomas, who seemed kind and put me at ease. There was some discussion about which class I should join, but that depended upon how much I already knew and the only way to establish that was to give me some kind of test. The questioning went on for most of the morning. I really didn't know what they were talking about and so responded in fear.

As I look back today through the mind of an adult, I can easily assess the situation. Here was a seven year old boy who had been desperately ill and had missed a great deal of schooling, who came from a poor family with very limited education and no track record or role models of success to act as a guide — and they expected him to respond with some ability for assessment! As far as I was concerned, the questions that they asked might just as well have been in Chinese. I was intimidated by the people and the surroundings did not enhance my confidence.

But the worst was still to come. After the

examination, which seemed more like an interrogation, I was taken to the junior class to be installed. I vividly remember the scene. The room had bare wooden boards and about 40 students were sitting in silence at their desks. Most were a little younger than me. In the front of the room was a raised wooden platform with a large table and a huge blackboard stretching from one side of the room to the other.

And then I saw her. She was a plump woman in her forties with small hands, hard eyes and dark hair that was pulled back tightly into a bun. She had the most severe appearance I had ever seen. This was my new teacher, Miss Phillips. She seemed to try and force a smile but couldn't quite make it. A discussion took place between the two adults and then I was ushered to a seat and into a relationship that was to have a lasting effect on my life.

Right from the start Miss Phillips and I did not get along. She seemed to continually direct questions to me that I could not understand, let alone answer! After only a few days I was to feel the full wrath of Miss Phillips. She asked me a question in front of the class, and I could not respond because I did not understand what she was saying. She slapped my face; then again, and again. I could not respond. She repeated the question and I said something that showed that I did not understand and was slapped again. Other children in the class were able to respond and knew what Miss Phillips was talking about, and yet I really couldn't comprehend and that infuriated her all the more.

I was to hate school and took every opportunity to stay away, sometimes feigning illness, at other times just going down to the park for the day until I was discovered, and then there was more trouble for me. During class Miss Phillips would often creep behind me and catch me looking into space, dreaming or drawing pictures rather than studying or absorbing the lessons and then she would fly into a rage and hit me either with her ruler or by hand. I was utterly confused because I really did not understand what was going on or comprehend what was being taught. Miss Phillips said that I was inattentive, dumb and naughty, but the real truth was I did not understand and, in fact, had never understood the simple rudiments of reading or writing and therefore did not comprehend the simplest lessons except for visualisations like drawing or stories that were read to me which I could hear.

The real crunch with Miss Phillips came over a particular lesson that she felt that I should have easily finished. By now it was far too late because she and I were on a permanent collision course and I did what she expected — upset her at any opportunity. I had made up my mind about one thing: Miss Phillips would never make me cry. She seemed to get a certain amount of satisfaction and a sense of victory if she could make a student cry and I had promised myself that she would never get that satisfaction from me.

Miss Phillips had changed tactics somewhat and in her efforts to either break my spirit or make me learn, she began punching me hard on the back or taking the point of my chin between her forefinger and thumb and banging my teeth together, which not only made me look ridiculous but gave her some kind of fulfilment because she always gave that strange smile after she had completed the act.

One unforgettable day, I did try extremely hard and passed my work up to Miss Phillips with a certain amount of pride and satisfaction, expecting at the very least a comment of acceptance or maybe even an acknowledgement of good work before the whole class. But Miss Phillips thundered down between the desks toward me and slapped my face, stood me up, shook me and punched my back and then finally took the point of my chin between her forefinger and thumb and shook with all her strength, yelling, 'Peter Daniels, you are a bad, bad boy and you are never going to amount to anything!'

That event both crushed and angered me and was to dog me for the rest of my school years. It affected my attitude and ability to the point where it became, in a sense, a self-fulfilling prophecy.

Over the last fifty years, I have witnessed many similar situations where people have been crushed, embarrassed, put down, criticised, limited, misunderstood and broken and it is to all those people that I am writing this book, so that they may come to realise that they can rise above anything. Limitations are like Olympic records — they are there to be broken!

We all come into contact with a Mr and Miss Phillips in life. They may have different names, they may come from different stations in life, they could even be someone close like a brother, sister, mother or father, relative, friend or stranger. They tell you 'it can't be done', 'the opportunities are not there'; 'the timing is all wrong'; 'you don't have the ability'. Miss Phillips can creep up on you or hound you continually; she will surprise you or enslave you. It can be a man or a woman or even a child; it can be circumstances, conditions or locations.

But as long as God continues to give breath to mankind, the unexpected will happen and to the surprise of some, the least may become the leader and the worst may become the best, and the poor may become rich. I have seen in my lifetime enough surprising achievements from what many would call the under-achievers to say with sincerity and vigor that the Mr and Miss Phillips's of the world are all wrong.

Today, of course, I fly around the world, live a

lifestyle of wealth, privilege and prestige, lecture to the great universities of the world on business attitudes, finance and management, act as a consultant to industries as one of the highest paid speakers in the world today, and see my books, cassettes and videos purchased by hundreds of thousands of people all around the world. I can say with proof and purpose:

'Miss Phillips, you were wrong!'

Miss Phillips, You Could Not Predict The Future

The outcome of what anyone predicts will not depend upon them but rather upon you.

Miss Phillips, You Could Not Predict The Future!

How often have you wanted to take up a new venture in business or some other field and someone has told you it will not work out? I am not talking about advice from an experienced person who has travelled the road but rather the predictions that come from people who rarely venture past the safe, shallow waters of comfort and mediocrity.

Many years ago my bank manager told me not to go into real estate because it was risky. If I had listened to his advice I would never have had the pleasures and the rewards of building a successful real estate business. I was told by a very prominent parliamentarian that I would never be a commanding speaker and yet today that is probably what I do best. Miss Phillips also said some things that have proven to be far from correct. I am sure that some advice that you have received over the years has also been proven wrong.

It seems to me there are three types of people giving advice:

1. Those who are experienced and should know.
2. Those who don't know, yet continue to give advice anyhow.
3. Those who may or may not know, but who have an ulterior motive.

Let's have a look at those three in order.

Firstly, those who are experienced and should know.

Often in my earlier years of struggle I sought an experienced adviser who could put me on the right track and show me the golden road to success. As I enquired and sought after such a benefactor, I found all too often that those who could help were either too busy or too fearful of competition to give assistance to someone else.

On one or two occasions an opportunity for dialogue with experienced, older men who had retired and who were prepared to give advice did arise, but usually they were so far removed from day to day activities that most of the comments they made were out of date or totally unrelated to what I was doing. As a matter of fact, I cannot recall any instance of good specific business advice for the future other than general principles of ethics, safety and hard work.

The other reason that you cannot get good

advice from those who should know is that they do not have a deep, measurable stake in the venture. To predict the future is a game of chance at the best of times and who wants to give advice and then be blamed for the results if they are wrong?

Secondly, those who don't know and yet continue to give advice.

This group of people is always coming up with suggestions. Why not do such and such? This is what I would do if I were you! What if this happens? And so it goes on. Sometimes negative, sometimes positive; sometimes they are friends or relatives, other times they are just those we meet along the road of life. They may have no stake in your life or they may have an interest, but there is very little validity in what they tell you because if you look at their own lives then you will generally see little evidence of great achievement that would substantiate their wisdom and give you any confidence.

These people are generally 'guesstimators', and will keep on giving advice, whether it be good or bad, because they have a real need to participate. On rare occasions they may give you some sound, accurate advice, but to be able to select that out of the enormity of other comments is no easy matter. On occasions I have asked these people to substantiate their right to offer such advice by detailing their experience or background, only to be greeted with a blank stare or a hostile remark.

Thirdly, those who may or may not know but have an ulterior motive.

Unfortunately there are those in every community who really do not want others to succeed. It may be because they sense that the other person has untapped ability and would create a formidable opponent. Or perhaps they feel others should learn the hard way and correct advice would only make them soft and lacking in tenacity. Of course, there are those who do not know, and they *know* that they do not know, but they give advice confidently, being unconcerned about the outcome.

Most advice given by those who have no stake in the final outcome is suspect.

The other type of advice that is given by those who know or should know is partial advice; it is enough to get you part of the way but no further. You have to return to the source of supply for the next step, which, of course, puts you under the complete control of your adviser. That is a very precarious position to be in.

The bottom line is that no one can predict the future. All business ventures are risks and if you are not prepared to accept risks then you have automatically removed yourself from the pathway to success. The Mr and Miss Phillips of this world who are prepared to predict the future, particularly in negative ways, will always be wrong because eventually all records *will* be broken, reset, and broken again. All markets will change and change again and new opportunities will arise continually.

Those who keep predicting the future are assuming a power that they do not have. In Bible times, if a prophet ever made a prediction that was wrong, he or she was killed because it was a definite sign of a false prophet. To make the present plus the past equal the future is a wrong mathematical equation and formulas for predictions are, at the best of times, suspect.

How then can you go confidently into the future or move into a new venture with any kind of assurance of success? It's difficult but not impossible; but it will require a great deal of thought. Of course, if you have a proven track record and you have experienced success already, you can and should be able to access situations quickly and accurately, but for those requiring advice, let me make some simple but effective suggestions.

1. Face the truth about yourself in respect to your ability, your motivation, your capacity to handle pressure and your ability to concentrate.

2. Seek out from non-theoretical sources information regarding the venture you are embarking on. This can come from government statistics, trade magazines and libraries. If you can get a position of employment in the industry for six months, all the better. Also seek out credit reference bureaus and find out how many com-

panies went broke in that particular field and enquire from the credit bureau and suppliers to those companies why they failed.

3. Prepare a dossier of valuable information in respect to your new venture, both positive and negative. Balance these against each other, bearing in mind that the final result, good or bad, will ultimately depend upon you and will fall upon your shoulders.

4. Create a goals program (see my book *How To Reach Your Life Goals*) with a time frame to get the job done. Monitor it regularly, assessing where you over- or under-estimated to help you make better decisions in the future.

Remember, that you alone are the future and there is no conscious future for you without your involvement. The outcome of what anyone predicts will not depend upon them but rather upon you, and you have the ultimate power because God has never robotised the mind of man but rather given him and her the power of choice. It is by choice, not chance, that success is created. Nobody can predict the future, but you have it within your hands to create it, shape it, and succeed in it.

PRINCIPLES

1. Do not allow others to hold power over you by their predictions.
2. Face the truth about yourself.
3. Remember, you are the future.
4. Life is choices not chances.

Miss Phillips, You Did Not Have The Final Authority

The only person who can exercise authority over your life is you.

Miss Phillips, You Did Not Have The Final Authority

When Miss Phillips said to me, 'Peter Daniels, you are a bad, bad boy and you are never going to amount to anything,' she assumed an authority that she did not have.

To have authority you must know a great deal about the matter under discussion. Otherwise, you are trying to use power without knowledge, which tends to do more harm than good. Miss Phillips made the mistake of leaping from school room authority to absolute authority without first earning that authority. This is not an uncommon mistake and it has been made by people with a much larger intellectual capacity than Miss Phillips, but that does not make it a valid, accurate, or authentic action.

The late, Dr. Albert Einstein was once quoted as saying that 'man only uses 10% of his mental ability'. Some time ago, when I was in San Jose,

United States of America, I had to speak to a very knowledgeable and intellectual audience. I dared to say that the great Dr. Albert Einstein was wrong. It drew a hushed response from the crowd, but I was on very solid ground. For Einstein to make his claim he would have had to be able to measure, with some accuracy, the capacity of the individual's human mind, and no one has been able to measure that, not even the great Dr. Albert Einstein.

As a matter of fact, even IQ tests only tell you where you are now and do not give any indication of your future potential. IQ tests are being severely questioned in relation to the real value of the results in respect to business success.

Always look for authority behind statements made about you or your future, particularly if they are negative. An authoritative negative remark has within its strong grip the capacity to withhold or restrict, whereas anything positive or encouraging has the power to uplift and expand.

I guess the most difficult remarks to handle, particularly if they are negative, are those which come from sources close to home. If your wife or husband, father or mother or an other close relative says something to you, it is much harder to ignore because they, above all others, have seen your best and worst; they have observed you over many years and in some ways have helped mould you into what you are now, and so they carry certain knowledge and facts about behaviour, moods, past deeds, attitudes and principles that you possess from which they form judgments.

Relatives or close companions also form opinions on the basis of their own fulfilled or unfulfilled dreams, disappointments and prejudices. These tend to colour their perspective on almost everything else they see or are involved in.

The fact that you have dreams and a desire to better yourself and that you feel unsettled about the status quo is in itself an indication that you can and should do something about it. But it will not be an automatic process. It will take perseverance and in many cases, pain and anguish, for that ability to be refined and come to the surface. As a Christian, I believe that the reason we feel so ill at ease and restless at times is that we were designed for a different kind of world, and one day we shall live in it.

Always remember that you are a unique human being. You cannot be duplicated or copied. Because you are so different from any other human being on this planet, then simple logic says you can make a unique contribution to the world. I repeat, no one else can be what you are and become what you can become.

I have often drawn a simple but provable conclusion in respect to the human race. Taken en masse, the behaviour of people is very often predictable. But on an individual basis, it is very unpredictable, and that is why the behavioural sciences can only act as a guide and will never be exact sciences.

Sometimes we find a person successful in his or her chosen field, but when they move to a different different or unrelated field of endeavour they fail miserably. Why do I include this comment? Only to alert you to the fact that success in one area does not automatically make you an authority in other areas.

Specific authority cannot be assumed; it must be earned. And specific authority cannot be automatically transferred to other areas of endeavour, whereas general principles can be.

One of the great tragedies of the western world today is that our politicians are given almost absolute authority over certain legislation, finance and industry, but they themselves have never run a business. After all, what is government but big business? I know of several cases of senators and other government leaders who failed miserably in business and are now in positions of authority in government, making big mistakes but able, through the cumbersomeness of government and bureaucratic red tape, to cover up their bunglings from the unsuspecting public.

Fortunately, errors of judgment or bad work habits and incorrect decisions are all too readily apparent to the budding entrepreneur, and so they should be. Because it is very often through bad judgment that good judgment is learned and, although trial and error may have its pitfalls and pains, it is still one of the more recognisable ways to achieve. The only person who can exercise authority over your life is you and it is by you and through you that growth and enterprise flourish. If you succeed, then those around you who are participating succeed with you; if you fail, then they, in a sense, have failed also.

If we accept that God has given us a free will, then we have to ask the question with vigor and candor, 'How dare anyone suggest that they can rule over our lives?' As long as we obey the laws of God and respect the rights of our fellow man, we can do whatever we want to do and go as far as we want to go, and our only limits are those that we place upon ourselves.

There is one final comment I would like to make before I close this chapter. If we are not going to accept limitations imposed on us by those who assume authority over us, what should our attitude be towards those who we feel do have obvious limitations? How do we relate to them? My answer is simple. Encourage, uplift, support, affirm and stimulate, because a person as you see them today is not necessarily the person you will see tomorrow.

Who would have dreamed that the obscure Adolf Hitler would shake the world or that the seemingly timid Mahatma Ghandi would defeat the British Empire, or that your average local pastor, Dr. Martin Luther King, would change the lives of the black people all over America and a bashful boy called Winston Churchill, who spoke with a lisp and could not get his arithmetic right at school, would be Chancellor of the Exchequer and through his dramatic speeches would mobilise a nation in great peril? Contemplate and take care! The insignificant person before you or inside you has the potential and sufficient latent authority over his or her life to achieve greatness.

Those who try to exercise authority over you are wrong!

PRINCIPLES
1. No one has been given ultimate power to rule over you.
2. No one has ever been able to measure the capacity of the human brain.
3. Affirm and encourage the nobody inside of you to become somebody.
4. The world has been challenged and changed many times by seemingly insignificant people and events.

Miss Phillips, You Did Not Understand The Problem

The problems that we have are very often not understood because we do not seek out the root cause of the problem.

Miss Phillips, You Did Not Understand The Problem

Problems, my friend Dr. Norman Vincent Peale says, are a sign of life. They teach character and develop growth. Now every problem raises questions which require answers if a solution is to be found.

Some people like to offer answers without ever hearing, let alone understanding the question! My problem with Miss Phillips was that I did not understand the question — so how could I possibly come up with an answer? In fact I only realised I had a problem by the way Miss Phillips reacted to me!

Miss Phillips did not enquire, evaluate or even guess what caused my problems, and therefore she was not able to appreciate the situation. It takes an understanding heart, a willing heart, a compassionate heart to search out a problem and solve it; it takes no heart to compound it.

Today you may have personal problems involving relationships and attitudes, or financial and maybe even physical problems. No solution will come unless the problem is understood.

Look into your background and upbringing for key phrases and cliches that have been part of your young and adult life and evaluate their validity and accuracy. Many families have one liners that go something like this: 'If you want to get ahead in this world, all you have to do is work hard and mind your own business', and yet I know, and I'm sure you do too, plenty of people who have done just that and are right on the breadline, with very little possibility of going any higher. They have been locked into a way of thinking that at best is incomplete and at worst, is totally wrong.

I could dig all my life with a pick and shovel, minding my own business, searching for gold — live a lonely, poor, heart-breaking and isolated life which benefited no one. On the other hand, I could spend some time in study and look at methods of detecting gold or refining it out of other deposits by careful analysis and continual searching; I could become very wealthy.

The problems that we have are very often not understood because we do not seek out the root cause of the problem, and until we do that we are only treating our difficulties in a superficial way and can never hope to grow, develop or over-come.

Likewise, we must seek out the root cause of problems in other people before we can be of any productive help to them.

The other part of this cliche is to 'mind your own business', and in effect it means not getting in-volved; and yet to succeed I believe that you *must* get involved not only in specific areas of com-mercial activity but also with the lives of in-dividuals, because business and growth *is* people and the more people skills you have, then generally the more business you will have.

Another cliche is: 'It takes money to make money'; yet I have seen people go into the networking business with virtually no money and become millionaires. In other words, search out the root cause of your problem and correct it, or learn to live with it and bear the consequences of it.

Some years ago, I wrote a very successful book called *How To Be Motivated All The Time*. In it I gave principles of motivation that would last a lifetime. I said that fear can be one of the greatest motivations in a positive or negative way. I have found that fear has many faces, including the fear of uncovering a problem that has become a crutch to lean upon or an excuse for lack of performance. During nearly a third of a century of involvement in business and philanthropic work around the world, dealing with people from all walks of life and of all ages, I have found that the fear of facing a problem was the most destructive force I have ever encountered.

If you have a blockage that is preventing you from doing the thing that you want to do or would like to do, then examine with honesty your fear level. Do you have protective barriers that need to be removed? Do you blame other people for your problems or blame the circumstances which you feel have been thrust upon you? That can act as a sinister but effective barrier that shields you effectively from putting your life on the line to be scrutinised in the clear uncompromising light of achievement.

You can start again and you can rise above circumstances whether they be financial, physical or emotional, and apply the great special power of strength that can only be obtained through a relationship with God Himself, because He does care — as you are His creation, you belong to His family!

Certainly, Miss Phillips did not understand my problem and other people may not understand yours, but you can analyse it yourself and turn your weaknesses into strengths and your vagueness into value. When seeking to help others, try to get to the real cause of the problem. This tends to be manifested only by the hostility or fear of the moment and might just be holding back a giant that, if released, could actualise dreams.

PRINCIPLES
1. Problems are signboards that indicate hidden treasures.
2. Problems understood act as keys to unlock giants.
3. Problems can be traced to early cliches and wrong information.
4. Problems are a growing part of life.

Miss Phillips, You Did Not Want to Help

No one can put you down and keep you down unless you let them.

Miss Phillips, You Did Not Want To Help

When Miss Phillips made that statement to me many years ago, she should have known that to condemn and criticise, to hurt, demean and poison a young mind is wrong. But I guess that was the climate of the times, and over fifty years ago teaching and child psychology were quite different. Miss Phillips might have been living out some of her own hurts, disappointments and frustrations. Who knows?

As I move through the parade of life, I see and meet many people who have been rejected and put down in many ways. It may have been something that happened early in life; for others it comes later. It may be rejection by a loved one or in a business arrangement. It does not matter where or when it happened, but *why* it happened is important.

If you have been rejected as a person of worth

and your self esteem has been shaken, or even annihilated, try to identify the accuser's motives. Next examine your own reaction. Then see whether even this negative event cannot be turned into a positive force for growth. Over the years many people have suggested that Miss Phillips probably did me a favour by condemning and criticising me. They say that gave me the drive and the will to succeed. I guess if we are to follow that logic, then we should reprogram our education system so that all children can have that benefit! Just imagine the opposite. If Miss Phillips had put her arm around me and sought to understand, encourage and help, who knows whether from that moment what talent I had might have manifested itself and I could have achieved a great deal more because of an early good start!

The Mr and Miss Phillips of this world put people down because they tend to operate from a closed mind-set which allows for no perspective other than their own; and, of course, unless they are intellectual geniuses, they will always miss the mark. When you understand that anyone who puts you down thinks this way, you are more able to handle the rejection because you understand that the centre is somewhat out of focus. The crucial point of the whole episode is to turn such rejection into self-help and thereby grow by the experience. How do you do this? Let me make some suggestions.

1. Realise that the person who has rejected you and really doesn't want to help is probably worse off than you. If we believe the Bible verse, 'Give and it shall be given unto you' (Luke 6:38), then we might, without any stretch of logic, suggest 'take and it will be taken from you'. As the person took away from you self-esteem and confidence and threw a spanner in the works of your dream-machine, then somehow they too have lost something of themselves, which may be more difficult to recover from. A closed mind not only excludes what others can do, but also excludes what you can do. It may pay to go back to that person and try to help them — in doing so you will help yourself even more.

I wish my Miss Phillips was alive today. I would go and help her, not by condemning or even reminding her of what she said, but rather to comfort her in her old age.

2. Having dealt with the accuser, let's deal with the content and ask some direct and pointed questions.

— Is it true?
— Was it in the correct context?
— Was it really meant to hurt?
— Was it used on others?

The first question: *Is it true?* In other words, when Miss Phillips said, 'Peter Daniels you are a bad, bad boy and you will never amount to anything', we have to look at the facts and answer with a resounding No, because without modesty or arrogance, the facts speak for themselves. Miss Phillips was wrong.

The person who has put you down and does not want to help you will also be wrong and may even have been proven to be wrong already.

The next question: *Was it in the right context?* When help is desperately needed and could be given by someone, that person has a responsibility to give some light. Instead there was rejection, and to a young boy starting off in life with a long future in front of him, and with other children looking on and listening who would be absorbing the message, the context was indeed wrong and really was never right.

The third question: *Was it really meant to hurt?* In my situation I could never really be sure about that except to say that it did hurt and it would have hurt Miss Phillips if someone had behaved that way towards her. But I venture to say that there may be some people who put others down and reject them without understanding or realising that they have hurt someone. That certainly doesn't lessen the pain of the recipient!

The final question: *Was it used on others?* My answer with regard to Miss Phillips is Yes, because I saw it happen all through my school years. As I moved out of her class, I saw it happening to other boys and girls. I find it interesting that in the decades that followed, I have observed many people of a similar nature who repeatedly put others down and refused help when they could have given it — in fact it seems that it was part and parcel of their lifestyle and was rarely challenged by the recipients.

Whether or not you really are in control of your attitudes and how you react will determine your progress or lack of it in the future. Many people I meet around the world from many different backgrounds and positions in society today are carrying and have been carrying the hurts and rejections of the past for many years. The great news is that you don't have to carry the opinions of others as scars upon your life because God gave you the ability to rise above them and grow in spite of them. Realise and accept that the greats of this world (and I have met many of them personally) have been rejected, put down, re-fused help and discarded and they stepped out of the quicksand of depression and low self worth into confidence and high self esteem, just as you can. No one can put you down and keep you down unless you let them because no one, except you, can control and determine your attitude to any situation.

Believe, because it's true, that you have enormous potential and accept that it can only be brought to the surface if you believe it can and endure the discipline necessary to make it happen. The Mr and Miss Phillips of this world may not want to help but you can help yourself by doing something nice for yourself today. You are your best friend!

PRINCIPLES:
1. Rejection can only hurt if we let it.
2. Your growth can be controlled by you.
3. You are your best friend.

Miss Phillips, You Only Had Your Own Perspective

Your critics and those who would put you down are always limited by their own perspective but you can create for yourself a perspective that is void of limitations.

CHAPTER FIVE

Miss Phillips, You Only Had Your Own Perspective

Just as the world, as seen through the eyes of a child, appears to be big and scary, so that which is seen by any human being appears to be different and is limited or expanded depending upon whose eyes and ears it is channelled through.

I like to move around people with empires in their brains because, as I plan strategies for the future and at times relate portions of my dreams and aspirations to them, so they will view it through their perspective and enlarge and expand my boundaries.

As a student of the behavioural sciences and a keen observer of the lives and behavioural patterns of others, I now understand that Miss Phillips looked at things from her own perspective. Miss Phillips was a school teacher and in the days gone by, that was a very prestigious profession. I can recall quite well that in those days, when you introduced a school teacher at any function or group, there was something of a mystique and an aura about that person, and the teacher's name was only mentioned in quiet, very respectful terms. It was assumed that a person teaching classes of children year after year would give each child exam marks which would in some degree indicate the kind of job that they were likely to get.

It was with this perspective that Miss Phillips made the predictions which still ring in my ears fifty years later; only now she is much better understood and, from my perspective, much easier to forgive. Always remember that the person who puts you down does so looking at you and your situation from his own perspective, which is limited or enhanced by his own relationships, experiences, exposure, hurts and dreams.

As I understand it, Miss Phillips had never ventured out beyond the district in which she lived and therefore did not have a world perspective. Any opinions or information about the world beyond were at best second hand and influenced by the perspective of others and therefore not as true as they would have been if they had been formed directly through the eyes, ears and emotions of Miss Phillips herself.

Miss Phillips had never gone into business and therefore could never have experienced the joy of success or the pain of failure in that field.

Miss Phillips had never raised a family — dealing first hand with the conflicts and difficulties which last well after the school bell has rung for the close of each day; nor had she enjoyed the deep love of a child of her own which melts the heart of every mother.

Miss Phillips had never taught above the infant class, which meant that her time was spent primarily with little children. So her mind was not stretched beyond the day to day activities. Her position, size, age, and attitude gave her a power that made her more feared than loved or admired.

That may have compounded any problems she may have had because in her own mind she could be right in everything.

Miss Phillips, it seemed, had never been ambitious; if she had she would have sought to move up the ladder in the Education Department. That did not happen, according to my later enquiries.

Maybe Miss Phillips' perspective was limited by her own expectations, but to transfer that limitation to those who were given into her care was to violate a trust.

By now you may be feeling very sorry for Miss Phillips and those like her. To me there is no room for sympathy. If my children or grandchildren were put down and limited by another person's perspective, I would be angry. To injure or cripple someone psychologically by accident or intent is

a very serious business and punishable by law;
but, it seems, to injure or cripple one's intellect by
accident or intent is excusable!

Of course, we must and should forgive those
who restrict, hurt and demean us because it is
much better for us. Forgiveness removes from our
lives an extra burden of grief. But to stand by and
allow it to happen to ourselves or someone else is
a matter for grave concern and immediate action.
My temper is usually under control, but if I see
someone talking down to someone else or if they
are trying to embarrass, ridicule or limit others,
and even myself, then I am afraid that on those
occasions, I have to step in and correct the
situation with some vigor.

Whenever you are criticised, limited or put
down by someone, recognise that person is re-
flecting his view of himself, and in a sense has
allowed you and all others who are involved to
gain insight into the deepest and most volatile
area of his own aspirations.

Understanding that a person's opinion or
comments are at least in part made up from their
own perspective leads me on to an additional
thought for you and it is this. Why not enlarge your
own perspective? How do you do this? Four
simple steps.

1. Believe that anything can be done by somebody — why not you?

2. Read biographies and build up a vocabulary

of information on overcoming incredible odds.

3. Become involved in helping others and affirming them. Choose twelve people you would like to meet and get to know who could stretch your mind and affirm your self-esteem.

4. Spend at least four hours a week in un-interrupted, concentrated thought about one area of your life. Search your subconscious and enter the deep recesses of your mind to bring out thoughts, ideas and perspectives that will not only change your life, but change the lives of others.

Your critics and those who would put you down are always limited by their own perspective, but you can create for yourself a perspective that is void of limitations.

PRINCIPLES:
1. The perspective of others may be okay for them, but it may not be alright for you.
2. Examine the reasons for the restricted per-spective others have before accepting what they say.
3. Expand and keep expanding your own per-spective and encourage others to do the same.

Miss Phillips, You Were A Bad Judge

Don't judge yourself too harshly because you aren't perfect; but you can change and improve.

Miss Phillips, You Were A Bad Judge

Lord Acton once supposedly said, 'Power tends to corrupt and absolute power corrupts absolutely.' Miss Phillips had power over her students and it could be said that she had almost absolute power.

During my travels around the world, the worst people to come into contact with in any country are customs officers. Anyone who has come up against these people will find no exaggeration in that statement. Why governments do not pay more attention to this area of the public service, which is the first impression given to a tourist or someone seeking to do business with their particular country, I do not know. But if you are stopped by customs, particularly in the western world, then you can expect to experience arrogance, rudeness, suspicion, power-holding and delays, particularly if you challenge their manner of speech or their *modus-operandi.*

What makes these people so offensive? It is the power placed in their hands without anyone on duty to see that it is not exaggerated. Or it is a lack of training in good manners and public relations. I am sure that from time to time customs officials *are* confronted with drug traffickers, terrorists and contraband purveyors, but the very large majority of visitors are expecting to find pleasant people, anxious for tourism and trade — not anticipating the overbearing antics of power-holders who flout their power at every opportunity.

Because of her position of almost total power, Miss Phillips was able to pass judgment on me without any defence council there to defend me and without any jury to validate a verdict. In doing so she adopted power over the weak and pronounced, as she thought, a life sentence of doom. (In some cases Miss Phillips has been proven correct in her judgment! A boy in our class has spent most of his life in prison and a great deal of it in solitary confinement.)

For someone to wear the judge's robe and pronounce a sentence of doom in your life is not only unfair but an act of sabotage of the worst possible kind. The number of lives that have made such judgments become self-fulfilling prophecies is too awesome to contemplate and the carnage and wastage of such words has left the whole world poorer because of it.

How many geniuses have been cut off before being allowed to grow? How many leaders have been stifled by such judgments and how many battered people have been created? How many lives have been lost to the timid waters of mediocrity or the dark doorways of crime because of statements made by those who do not know or because of people who use their positions of power incorrectly or inadvisedly?

I suppose what we are really talking about here is fair play. In fair play there is a certain amount of give and take which gives all concerned an opportunity to be heard and allows a just decision to be made. When someone says to you, 'It can't be done', or 'You'll fail', or 'You're getting too big for your boots', or 'The timing is wrong', then they must be prepared to put their own lives up for scrutiny. There appears to be a lot of loose, negative talk which does not come from an informed source but rather is based on ideas plucked from the air or taken from the state of one's digestion.

Negative statements must be supported by hard evidence; we are being just as foolish when we let them pass by without comment or challenge.

How often does it happen in business meetings where a decision about something has to be made that someone will say, 'I'm not sure about this'! That one statement can cause all discussion

to cease and prevent any movement or growth —
without any validating reasons! When I am
chairing a Board meeting and that kind of remark
is made, I will often say, 'Ignore that remark unless
it is validated by substance', because to advertise
you don't know something is to advertise your
deficiency, and who really wants to do that?

To make judgments takes a great deal of
experience, knowledge and wisdom. I am re-
minded of an acquaintance of mine who became a
lawyer and finally went into his own business. He
developed that law firm to a point where it was
respected and successful and, as recognition of
his ability to formulate and practice good law over
twentyfive years, he was made a judge in the
Supreme Court with the power to judge others.
The question that needs to be asked of those who
continually judge others is, what kind of experience have they had in making accurate
assessments and what great undertaking have
they successfully built that qualifies them to tell
you something cannot be done? What we need to
do, of course, is to know and study our own
industry or endeavours so that if we are called on
to make judgments, they will be made with
accuracy and not by guess work. But to stand in
judgment of someone's future, not knowing what
the future holds, or how an individual may act or
react in any given circumstance, is expecting too
much because of our own inability to measure the

capacity and the tenacity of another person.

Give helpful advice by all means, offer counsel if you can see that someone is heading in the wrong direction, but offer and give transparently, acknowledging that you are not infallible and that you don't have the final responsibility. If the person chooses to go in a different direction, then wish them well and Godspeed as they attempt to blaze new pathways of adventure in life; if they fail, comfort, encourage and esteem them so that they might try again. Assure them that the only time they really fail is when they give up.

In my lifetime, I have found that the chase and the pursuit are far more fun and give far more exhilaration than the acquisition because after the acquisition the adventure of life looks for new horizons. You can even start to looking for new horizons when the finish line is in sight.

Don't judge yourself too harshly because you aren't perfect; but you can change and improve, so be careful of judging others. Don't be a Miss Phillips.

PRINCIPLES
1. Be careful of the power-holders.
2. Examine judgments for validity based on experience and research.
3. Be benevolent in judging others.
4. Don't judge yourself too harshly.

Miss Phillips, You Did Not Recognise The Uniqueness Of Every Human Being

What makes a person unique is not what they do as much as who they are.

Miss Phillips, You Did Not Recognise The Uniqueness Of Every Human Being

What Miss Phillips did many years ago and what happens even today when pronouncements and limitations are put on people is that the individual's destiny is denied, a destiny shaped by the unqiueness of every human being.

We all seem to have checks and balances. Some people are good at theory, others are more pragmatic; some are musical, others are athletic; while some seem to be multi-talented, others appear to be less talented.

What makes a person unique is not what they do as much as who they are. Each person is a child of God made in the likeness of God, but individual and separate from anyone else on the face of the earth.

You react differently to given circumstances, and you feel differently from others whether you are happy, sad, angry or in love. You are unique in the universe and no one is ever going to feel, think, react, dream, or do the things that you are capable of. Once you accept that we are all different, then it follows that your uniqueness must show itself in your lifestyle and abilities.

There are three things that I am really sure about in respect to the uniqueness of every human being:

1. We have latent talents that may never be brought to the surface if the need or opportunity does not present itself.

2. We are multi-talented, that is, every individual has many talents.

3. We have special talents which are quite unique to us. The way they are expressed will also be unique.

Let's examine each one of those three suggestions in a little more detail.

We have latent talents. It sometimes amazes me to see obviously gifted people perform. They do a multitude of tasks extremely well, but with seemingly little effort, while others look on and marvel at their deeds.

Is it true that there are specially gifted people who possess such extraordinary ability that they defy the notion of the equality of mankind? Think of two pianists. Is the concert pianist who reaches the dizzy heights of world acclaim more gifted because he or she does not have to persevere as hard as the equally world famous pianist who still has to practise every day to maintain that world class standard of performance? I would like you to consider that both are probably gifted equally because their performance is the same. One has a more prominent gift of understanding music whilst the other has to rely on his or her more prominent gift of discipline.

The famous birdman of Alcatraz was put behind prison bars for life because of a violent crime. It was said of him that he was amoral and not fit to be allowed to go back into society. But the long time he was to endure in incarceration caused him to discipline his life in concentrated thought and he became a genius in many areas of academic life.

We are multi-talented. During World War II there were many young men and women who were taken out of professional life and literally thrown into different countries of the world. They had to face challenges that earlier would have seemed impossible to cope with. Not until we have our back to the wall or until we are faced with an unusual opportunity, or confronted with a major crisis, do we have any perception of what we are capable of doing. When someone suggests that your talents are limited or that you are moving out of your field of expertise, what they are really observing is that you have not yet been given the opportunity, inspiration or difficulty that is necessary to bring whatever talents there are hidden beneath the surface to reality.

We have special talents that are unique to ourselves. When you consider the uniqueness of every human being — their colouring, features, finger prints, height, weight and mental perception — is it not reasonable to assume that, as we are different and special in these ways, we may also have different and special talents which are exclusively ours? It is not hard to see that all great and famous painters, sculptors and vocalists look and sound entirely different. Whilst we can be trained to behave in the same way, and many do copy someone else either deliberately or unconsciously, we still have a uniqueness of thought, expression and feeling that can show itself in a unique gift which is exclusively ours.

The question that now becomes paramount in our minds is: How do I find my special talent? And when I find it, how can I develop it to the full?

To find a special talent with unique qualities requires not so much hard work but disciplined dreaming. Most of us live our own lives in wishful thinking, never expecting our dreams to become reality. Our dream machine is really running without direction or purpose.

We have this gift of life only once. As you live you spend or trade it for the activities you get involved in, the challenges and opportunities you seize or miss. At the end of your life, what you have done during those years is what you have traded your life for.

Why not take a day or two or even a week off to get alone and dream and think of what you would really like to trade your life for! In the beginning you will find it quite scary and difficult to discipline your dream machine, but persevere until your dream becomes what you want it to do or be. Your dreaming, I believe, will reveal your talents and uniqueness in the shape of what you really need in order to realise the dream.

To develop your talents, I would suggest an in-depth study of my book *How To Reach Your Life Goals*. Be prepared to exercise discipline and endure some pain and heartache, because just as a marathon runner endures pain and must very often pass the pain threshold to get his second wind, so unique talents are sometimes hidden deep within a person and to bring them out may hurt.

The individuality that you and everyone else has puts a brand, as it were, on every human being and confirms that God's stamp is on the universe. Accept your uniqueness and be prepared to develop your talents into the greatness you can and should be to the glory of God Himself.

Step forward and upwards and be recognised — you are unique in the universe and you have no duplicate.

PRINCIPLES

1. You are uniquely gifted and talented.
2. Dream, and discover your special gifts.
3. Be prepared to dig deep and endure the discomfort of the surfacing and living out of your uniqueness.

Miss Phillips, You Were Biased

Control and program your attitude on the basis of positive reinforcement that will reflect itself in your conscious and unconscious thoughts.

Miss Phillips, You Were Biased

Any newspaper you scan, any film you see, any book you read (including this one) is biased.

I am, for instance, biased towards biblical truths and absolutes, and biased towards the free enterprise system, and biased towards the seemingly unlimited possibilities of the individual.

So you will find that those who are negative and those who power-hold or pull you back, put you down or seek to limit your growth, have a particular bias. Miss Phillips was biased.

In seeking to understand bias we come up with some very enlightening discoveries.

1. Whenever we are confronted with a negative bias, we find it difficult to avoid its power because a negative bias is always stronger than a positive bias. Negative thinkers rarely call for evidence to support their position; if they do, the evidence is, at best, elusive and, at worst, not demonstrable.

2. A positive bias generally carries with it the need for proof. That can complicate matters and

very often brings in other issues from opponents which tend to obscure the point in question rather than clarify or confirm it.

3. A bias for or against something without a living philosophy or some provable principles or evidence is the arch enemy of freedom and opportunity. The bias that Miss Phillips had was particularly wrong because she was charged with the solemn, serious and responsible task of moulding the minds and programming the future of the young. The use of personal bias or a power bias in that situation goes totally against the ideals of the teaching profession.

Sometimes, bias is just bad thinking, or even speech without thought. That does not lessen the damage, make it excusable or minimise the hurt, but rather makes the act more irresponsible and the person delivering the comment less credible.

A famous illustration of bias or opinion without serious thought is Bishop Wright. Many years ago he stated quite categorically that man would never be able to fly in the air. Yet his sons, Wilbur and Orville, were the first to demonstrate manned flight!

Teachers and college professors used to say emphatically that what goes up must come down. Today, of course, we understand that sputniks and aero-space waste and obsolete material may continue to orbit in space forever.

It was said in sporting circles that man would

never break the four minute mile in running; that was proven wrong by Roger Bannister and has been proven wrong thousands of times since. These examples ought to give us all a serious warning to re-evaluate our thoughtless and careless biased remarks.

So how can you cope with other people's biased opinions and criticism and effectively turn them into positive reinforcement for your life, to propel you on to whatever challenge faces you either now or in the future? The obvious answer, of course, is to control and program your attitude on the basis of positive reinforcement that will reflect itself in your conscious and unconscious thoughts and thereby cause actions towards growth in your daily life. Here are some simple principles.

1. Have a series of short, medium and long term goals which are very clearly defined with deadlines and measurements.

2. Put the basis of your goals onto a card which you can carry in your wallet or purse for easy and continued accessibility. Read it daily and refer to it particularly at those moments when you have doubts.

3. Keep a record on a cassette tape of your feelings and attitudes when things go well for you and play it back when doubt creeps in.

4. Read good biographies and inspirational books and listen to a range of motivational tapes to keep the flow of positive reinforcement at a

continuing level. Remember that you were created with a bias towards success, with the image of God overshadowing your life. Under such an awesome shadow, you can do, be and make out of your life that which you are fully prepared to believe in and work towards.

Why not, starting today, enourage the bias that is already within you by resolving never to allow the bias of others to interfere or misdirect the image of God within you.

Your future is your very best friend, irrespective of what has happened in the past. It waits for your dreams to be translated into action to provide you with all the joys, wealth, giving and self esteem you desire. The only difference between poverty and riches, low self-esteem and high self-esteem is the fulfilment of a dream that has within its strong, tightly held frame the commitment to bring it to mature reality. Your personal bias is for your protection and it can act as a stimulant to your dream machine which will come to your consciousness from time to time, provoking you to do something great that will demonstrate that you are here for a purpose. The purpose is singularly yours. This bias of other people which they seek to thrust upon you is exclusively theirs, and should never intimidate you or misdirect your course from the aspirations and dreams that belong to you.

Be a winner and retain your individuality by

focussing on the productivity and ingenuity that belongs to you. Reject the bias of others. That may be all right for them, but you march to a different drummer!

PRINCIPLES

1. Remember the negative bias is always stronger than the positive bias because it rarely calls for evidence to support its position.
2. Bias is the arch enemy of freedom and opportunity.
3. Focus on the positive bias in yourself and become a winner.

Miss Phillips, You Presumed Too Much

Presumption is little more than a bad guess and is very often used as a substitute for facts.

Miss Phillips, You Presumed Too Much

Presumption is little more than a bad guess and is very often used as a substitute for facts. How often have you presumed and been wrong? I know I have and it was because I tried to 'guesstimate' on the basis of feelings and fuzzy thinking. You are rarely right!

Other people will presume upon you, but what they see may not be what they get. The Chancellor of Germany, Adolf Hitler, in 1939 through his ambassador in London, England, tried to intimidate the late Sir Winston Churchill, when he made ultimatums to him in respect to Europe and Germany's demands. The Germans at that time had presumed that because England appeared to be managed by an old and flabby group of aristrocrats, they were incapable of presenting any resistance to the might and discipline of the German army. Sir Winston Churchill reponded that judgment must not be made on England as it appeared to be but rather as it *could* be under threat. Then they would respond with determination and resolve. Of course, he was proved to be correct.

People may see you now and presume on the basis of observations of your past and present situation; but they cannot predict how far you could go if you were under threat and made a strong resolution to respond. Over the years you may have allowed people to presume on you and against you and in return you may have responded as was expected; but that need not always be the case. Allowing others to presume on you is giving up your God-given right to be all that you can and want to be as a response to this opportunity we call life.

How dare anyone presume against you without recourse! How dare anyone tell you that you are limited! How dare anyone suggest to you that they know the capacity and strengths of your character!

When Miss Phillips presumed, many years ago, against a 7 year old boy, then she in fact presumed against herself because for every action there is an equal and opposite reaction. Her presumption, now proven wrong, will provoke others to presume against her, and they will imagine all kinds of possibilities against her character.

Many people have been shackled for a lifetime by the presumption of others. Those who hold this power play on the insecurity of others by taking up a position of superiority, thereby making the victim feel, in a sense, subject to them. There are some simple rules for combatting presumption against you.

1. Look at the intimidation factor in your life. Are you easily intimidated by others? If so, you need to affirm yourself daily. This can be satisfactorily done by writing out a clear, concise paragraph or two about your strengths — not overlooking weaknesses but realising that your strengths are of value and your weakness can be strengthened. Say it aloud, two or three times a day, even record it and play it as you drive. Affirm a belief in your own value as a person.

2. Anyone suffering from intimidation should take a course in public speaking, or, better still, become a commission salesperson, which will thrust you before others and allow you to learn to combat other people's influence. I particularly suggest commission selling because it cannot be faked or sidestepped or covered over — you get paid in direct proportion to your willingness to confront and convince. There is no better measurement that I know.

3. Accept the presumption or intimidation as a dare and adopt an 'I'll show you' attitude. Declare

war on the issue, and with perseverance and careful planning, commit yourself to overcome and succeed.

4. Do not let people treat you as an invisible person by allowing them to presume against you continually without response. There is a time for a show down. Call for facts and a stop to the foolish talk that binds others. Go to the person and tell them how you feel and what they are doing to you and others and ask them to consider what their irresponsible behaviour does to limit other people.

Next time someone presumes against you and your future, do not get hurt, or retaliate, do not withdraw or accept their presumptions, but rather, use the situation as a catalyst to propel you, excite you and encourage the greatness within you. Remember that you have a place in the universe and you deserve to be here because within your veins pumps the strong red blood of those who have gone before you. In time to come you can demonstrate to all those who dared to presume against you that your value as a person is not measured by what others say, but rather by your response to the trials and triumphs of life.

Whatever life span you have left, you can make a contribution towards the world by acting as a role model for others, either in achievement, patience, love, kindness or by just hanging in there when others give up. Dwelling on the way in which others view your life and presume to control or limit you will not be the acid test in the end, but rather your own commitment to triumphing over adversity and towards making the world a better place will be.

PRINCIPLES

1. Do not let anyone control you by presumption.
2. Do not be an invisible person, but speak up when you are presumed against.
3. Remember that the blood that pumps in your veins was tested in the battle of life before you came along and is your heritage.

Miss Phillips, You Had A Limited Vision

If I were to name the most important ingredient in achievement and success, it would have to be vision.

Miss Phillips, You Had A Limited Vision

It is not lack of education that stops people from getting ahead. It's not lack of opportunity either that prevents growth. It's not family influence or the lack of it that sets you on the pathway of life. It is rather lack of vision.

If I were to name the most important ingredient in achievement and success, it would have to be vision. The Bible goes even further, saying, 'Without vision, the people perish'. Call it what you will — dreaming, visualisation, goals, a magnificent obsession, it all amounts to the same thing: somewhere to go and something to do that excites the imagination to the point that plans and action follow. I guess you could sit all day for years and dream about a better marriage, wealth and a deeper spiritual experience, fame or great works and at the end of your time, realise with wonder that nothing happened. Well, the simple answer to that is — dreams don't work unless you do. Dreams and visions of the future only tell you what is possible and what you are capable of doing, but it is up to you to put legs and arms on your dreams and make them into a working reality.

Someone once asked me to define the word success and my reply was 'a willingness to bear pain to achieve a mighty purpose'. I am sure that others might have a better cliche, or a more descriptive explanation, but my analogy has certainly satisfied my thoughts and experiences of success. Sometime, if not already, someone is going to limit your vision by suggestions or ridicule and maybe even by a sincere concern for your well being, but only you can turn off your dream machine; you are the only one that can actually activate the switch. Your dream machine will persist in working only on rare occasions if it is not acted upon and then eventually through lack of use it will roll over and die.

To live with a vision of the future which is full of optimism, challenge, risk and purpose, is living life to the full; without the thrill of adventure and the excitement of the chase, life can become a steady, unhappy walk to a waiting grave with nothing left behind to act as a catalyst to challenge others.

You may have already felt the cold, damp blanket of despair and discouragement placed upon you, as I felt it so many years ago when Miss

Phillips tried to limit my vision. Perhaps you are starting to understand something of the way the influence of others can limit you. If that is the case, then please let me explain something to you.

When other people seek to limit you and you allow them to do it, there are two things that will happen. First, by allowing your vision to be limited, you have abandoned your personal sovereignty, crushed your possibilities for the future and stunted your growth. Second, your oppressor has suddenly been elevated because (a) you have obeyed, (b) you are no longer a threat to his feeling of superiority and (c) you have been successfully put down.

Generally speaking, the person who talks you down or criticises your dreams has set his own course and has limited himself. If you realise your dreams then you pass him and thereby expose his limitations.

One of the greatest privileges I have as I move constantly around the world, is to speak and share thoughts with some of the world leaders in areas of religion, business, government and art. Sometimes it is at business meetings and at other times it is by personal invitation or over a meal. During these times, when the opportunity presents itself, I ask questions about their early life, their struggles and achievements. Sometimes I take notes and occasionally use a tape recorder to capture some of the rare talent that is exposed during these meetings. When the main discussion is over and everyone is relaxed and quite comfortable, I usually ask a special question: 'Do you have any regrets?' Without exception (although these world leaders in their fields may have used different words) they have said that they 'did not think big enough!'

Imagine, if you will, these giants of the twentieth century who have done what many would say was impossible, confessing that they did not think big enough. In other words, their biggest limitation was their own lack of vision.

One of these people explained it this way. 'If I had known I could have come this far, then I would have dreamed bigger!'

Today, as I speak on the platforms of the world and stand for hours signing autographs and see the books and videos and cassettes that God has permitted me to produce being shipped and purchased around the world, I am continually provoked by the question — am I thinking big enough? Don't let anyone limit your vision by telling you that you're getting too big for your boots, or that you can't do it, but rather ask yourself the question, 'Am I thinking big enough and am I prepared to endure the pain to make my dreams a reality?'

PRINCIPLES
1. Limited vision means limited life.
2. With limited vision you will never see the full picture.
3. Do not allow anyone to destroy your dreams.
4. Without vision the people perish.
5. Dreams don't work unless you do.

Miss Phillips, You Were Negative

One of the most powerful forces in overcoming negativism is the ability to have some discipline over the subconscious mind.

CHAPTER ELEVEN

Miss Phillips, You Were Negative

The man who invented the Polaroid instant camera said, 'Whenever I get a good idea, I insulate myself from negative thinking people because I only need one negative comment to destroy a good idea.'

Negativity destroys whereas positive thoughts develop and expand the human mind and challenge all things to the limit. The negative influences of other people's thoughts can crush your spirit and push you aside from the giant within you.

I was watching television one day; a middle-aged couple were being interviewed on a current affairs program. They had recently been divorced and the man was asked what he felt the cause of the marriage breakup was. He replied that he could never get anything done because his wife would not agree on jobs, moves, holidays, outings; she was basically negative on most things. The woman (his recently divorced wife) said that being negative put her in control, and that is what gave her the most satisfaction. When asked why she felt in control, the woman remarked with gusto, 'Anyone who is negative in a relationship always has control because they have the power to withhold. The other person eventually gets tired and gives up'.

How often have you given up when the negative comments of others were thrust upon you? How often have you discarded thoughts that seemed good at the time, but, because of a negative comment by someone else, you discarded it? How often when you could see a light at the end of the tunnel and there was little else to do but hang on, a word of discouragement or negativity was given to you and it cut the ground from beneath your feet?

Nobody grows under a negative influence, just as nobody can grow without positive input. The Mr and Miss Phillips of this world will never go away because a negative pivot point acts as a base for control of others. Rarely does negativism accept within its tightly held frame the elements of responsibility. People do not grow under a negative influence because it stifles growth, discourages risk and suppresses great thoughts. On the other hand, a positive mental attitude enhances the gifts of the individual and presupposes success and growth.

Next time anyone becomes negative towards

you and your ideas, quickly ask yourself the question, 'Am I in control of my thoughts and thereby of my life?' Or, 'Am I subject to the negative barbs of those around me?'

Negativity always binds the receiver and gives control to the sender. The control of your life must remain within the domain that God placed it, namely the individual, and under that control you can be catapulted to the dizzy heights of fame, fortune and understanding. Be optimistic about the future and the role that you have to play in it, irrespective of your age or position at the moment. An optimistic view of the future, together with good plans and a will to work at it, can change any situation for the better.

Most people think that if they are fifty or sixty years of age, it is too late for an optimistic outlook for the future; yet Ray Crock, who developed McDonald hamburgers, Colonel Sanders, the Kentucky Chicken king and JC Penny of the department store fame, and many others show that it is not so. These men went through incredible misfortunes, disappointments, illnesses and ridicule, but, by ignoring all setbacks, negativity and misfortune, they bounced back and became successful, and so can you.

As I travel around my own country and around the world, I see great monuments to individual achievement that demonstrate the capacity of the human spirit; but, in all of my observations, I have not yet seen a statue, plaque or memorial of any kind dedicated to negativism.

Looking for the positive in a situation puts you in control, but allowing negativity to take over is a surrender to the circumstances of the moment and produces frustration, fear, worry and failure. Most negativism is produced by fear which is probably one of the most powerful motivators known to man, and because fear is so powerful, it tends to disrupt positive thought and stifle enterprise. Fear usually comes from the imagination, although direct fear is a result of visible or immediate danger and is a means of protecting us against harm and therefore should be acknowledged as a positive rather than a negative force.

However, most fear comes from the imagination of what could happen if everything went wrong. Therefore, one tends to major on protection to the extreme to the point where it is out of control and you are reacting to circumstances that have not and may never take place.

It is good for us to bear in mind that the subconscious cannot tell the difference from a real or imagined act. Let me explain further. If you are having a nightmare and something is chasing you, or you are under threat in your dream, then your mouth goes dry, your heart beats faster and even your legs and arms move slightly. Nothing has really happened, but the results would be similar if it were actually happening!

One of the most powerful forces in overcoming negativism is the ability to have some discipline over the subconscious mind and this can be done by developing your imagination. A world famous entrepreneur I know spends 45 minutes a day imagining what he wants to happen in his life. He does it without fail every single day.

One final word on negativity. Develop your sense of humour and learn to laugh regularly. I believe laughter is an instant holiday and provides quick relief from tension.

PRINCIPLES
1. Negativity destroys — positivity builds.
2. Negative remarks always bind the receiver and give control to the sender.
3. Laughter and imagination can turn negative imaginings into positive realities.

Miss Phillips, You Will Always Be Wrong

The Mr and Miss Phillips of this world will always be wrong because the human spirit with each heart beat pushes against the odds.

CHAPTER TWELVE

Miss Phillips, You Will Always Be Wrong

This book primarily concerns my own personal experiences, but do not imagine that it is a special or isolated case. What has happened in my life can and has been repeated in all walks of life all around the world.

The Mr and Miss Phillips of this world will always be wrong because the human spirit, with each heart beat, pushes against the odds. Just as every mountain, sea and air space will be challenged by man, so will the inner space of the human mind, which, at this stage, is a mystery to us all.

Psychologically mankind is in its early infancy. Many have tried to unlock the doors of the mind and reveal its secrets by mysticism, and charlatans of every kind have made and will always make promises that cannot be fulfilled; at their worst they cause damage to the recipients and, at best, provide little relief or hope.

I guess that pseudo-psychological mumbo-jumbo of some sort will always pull in those who are looking for a quick fix or an ultra-disciplined lifestyle that provides a feeling of security. All seriously minded psychologists and behavioural scientists believe that you cannot help anyone unless they want to be helped and are prepared to be involved by way of personal commitment.

Beware of quackery and promises of the easy ways (which are usually expensive) or the commitment to a guru who controls your very existence. The simple truth is that those who tell you that you can't change are wrong. People do change and can achieve, but it does take commitment and at times you may need help. We will of course always have with us the authoritative group who somehow get their own sense of self worth by controlling others.

Those who seek to hold power either by their position or by their predictions will always be wrong because you cannot harness the human spirit for any length of time.

On my office wall I have a chart that shows 8,000 years of human history with events and changes of power, wars, special events and special people; but most of all it shows the resilience of the human spirit and the continued resistance to power-holders. The ultimate authority over you is yourself because God has given you a free will to choose; but what you do with that free will may cause you to be accountable, not only to yourself but to those around you and to the provider of that free will.

Authoritative figures come and go and their predictions towards those they try to rule over are always limited because no one can rule over your dreams. So you can experience in your own imagination just how something could be, rather than how it is.

A dear friend of mine, Tom Tipton, was once asked how he coped during the dark days of segregation as a black man in the United States. Tom replied, 'I did not have a ghetto mentality but rather looked at all men made in the image of God.' Humanly speaking, I guess, we would want to lash out at those who presume to rule over us by their attitude, actions or desires; but human beings are so unpredictable and so unique, it is almost impossible to categorise. Anyone who has been in a management position or has served the public can vouch for the fact that, humanly speaking, people are different and that difference has little or no pattern except in special circumstances were boundaries, for some reason or other, exist. Spiritually, of course, all boundaries vanish and for anyone to try and constrain, restrict or imprison the human spirit is like trying to control the wind or the sea.

Our spirits soar one day and fall the next and our

emotions are often like the state of our digestion and have a poor track record of reliability. But it is necessary to feed the spirit because as it is fed so it is energised. George Mueller, who founded orphanages many years ago, lived well into his latter years. Someone once asked him how he was able to continue on so late in life and his reply was, 'I gain my strength from the recuperating powers of the Bible'. So we all must find that which invigorates our spirit, which in turn helps not only our energy level, but provides the oil to lubricate our dream machine. Who has not been broken of spirit or bereft of hope? We all have at some time or other and it's then that the spirit that is within needs to be revitalised and stimulated.

The final action that can be performed by you to create the spirit, the power, the optimism and the dreams to provoke and push you forward is the key that we have mentioned and referred to so often in this book. It is the power of choice, which after all is the integrity of the soul. A track to run on or a belief system: call it what you may, but, finally, the spirit within has to have a reason to act and keep on going for growth to be realised. Many people become sluggish and dry of spirit when confronted with disappointments and failures, but a belief in who you are and your purpose for being and an honest commitment to that belief will keep you going until all is accomplished.

The Mr and Miss Phillips of this world will

always be wrong, psychologically, humanly and spiritually because they cannot tap into or measure your unlimited and undiscovered potential.

PRINCIPLES
1. The human spirit defies limitations.
2. The human spirit needs constant stimulation.

Miss Phillips, You Forgot God

The Mr and Miss Phillips of this world will always be wrong because they forget the God factor.

CHAPTER THIRTEEN

Miss Phillips, You Forgot God

For the finale of this book and for the last time I have to share with you via this medium, I want to leave with you some closing challenges and encouraging thoughts.

Human history has demonstrated that people can change, circumstances can change and even countries can change. In the course of human events the unexpected seems to happen. There is a great deal of truth in the saying, 'Be nice to the people on the way up because you meet the same people on the way down'. Those who are in power today, are out of power tomorrow and as you look back on human history the only real permanence in events is change.

Some years ago my wife and I were visiting Manila in the Philippines and suddenly we found ourselves in a revolution. Within a few short days, the then leader, President Ferdinand Marcos, was deposed and fled into exile and a seemingly shy widow became the ruler of that country. The change from the flower power of the hippies in the late 60's to the yuppies of the 80's emphasises again the dramatic change in human history. Changes can be dramatic and permanent and what seems to be in fashion one day can be out of fashion the next. Human beings can change quickly and I have seen some remarkable examples of this in my lifetime that would sound like story book novels rather than real life examples.

The exciting news is that *you* can change dramatically, permanently and with confidence. You need not live a life of fear, uncertainty and with low self-esteem. As a matter of fact, your change can be so special that some would dare to call it a miracle. Let me suggest what type of change can be made.

1. You can be reassured about your future and your past can be put behind you.

2. You can have security amidst any crisis.

3. You can have peace in a world of turmoil.

4. You can have God as your father.

It happened to me many years ago and it revolutionised my life and helped me to understand my destiny before God and my role here on this earth. It happened when I gave my life to Jesus Christ and made Him my Lord and Saviour forever.

The same experience can be yours as you prove to the world your uniqueness. You can change the world because you have filled the God vacuum within you with dynamic life that gives strength to the weary, wisdom to the simple and power to the weak.

Yes, the Mr and Miss Phillips of this world will always be wrong because they forget the God factor.